Where does food come from?

30040000318972

Photography by Bill Thomas

Illustrations by Elise Fowler

A lot of our food
comes from plants.

Vegetables,

fruits,

and some seeds are food.

They all come from plants.

Plants grow in the ground.

Plants have roots,

stalks,

and leaves.

Plants have flowers,

fruit,

and seeds.

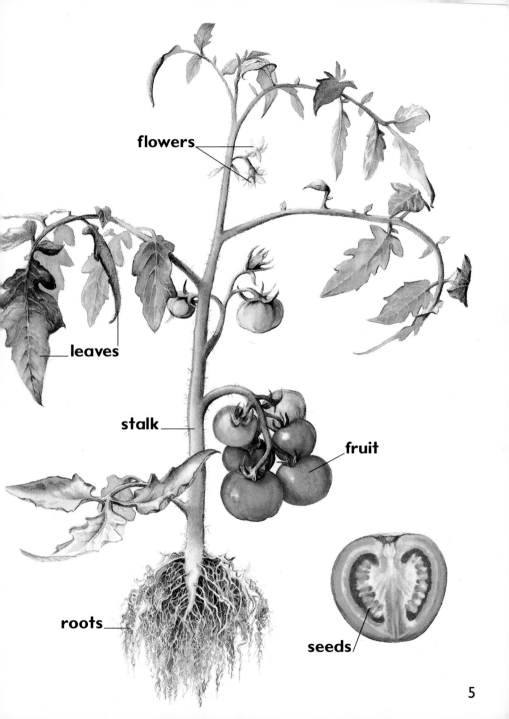

flowers

leaves

stalk

fruit

roots

seeds

5

Some vegetables grow
on top of the ground.

cabbage   **lettuce**   **spinach**

We can see them growing.

Some vegetables grow under the ground.

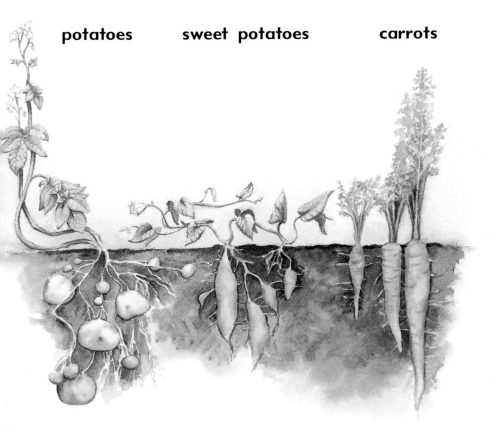

potatoes   sweet potatoes   carrots

We can not see them growing.

Some vegetables
have stalks
that we can eat.

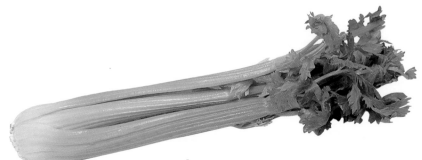

celery

asparagus

Some vegetables
have flower buds
that we can eat.

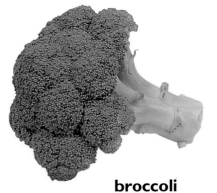

broccoli

cauliflower

Some fruits grow on trees.
We can see the fruit
getting bigger and bigger.

apple

Some fruits grow on the ground.
When the fruit is ready,
we can eat it.

pineapple

watermelon

We eat the seeds
of some plants.
Peas are seeds,
and they grow inside pods.

We cook the seeds of some plants before we eat them.

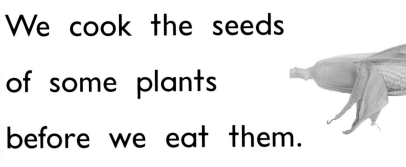

These seeds can be made into flour.

wheat

rice

corn

Lots of foods are made from flour.

bread

pancakes

pasta

chapattis

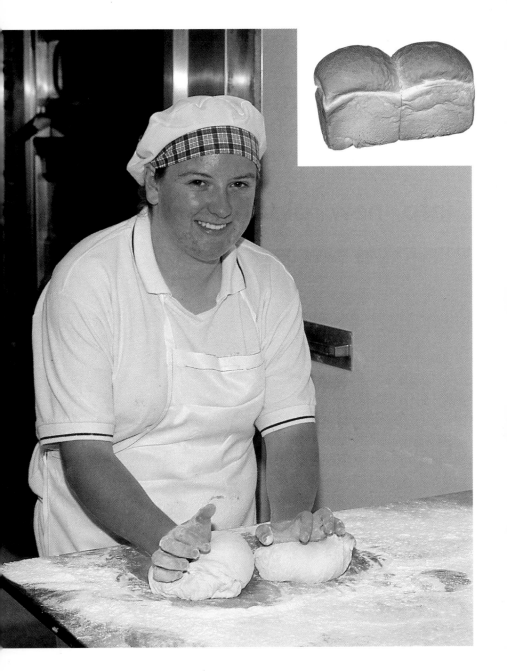

We put some of the seeds
back into the ground.
The seeds will grow
into new plants for us to eat.